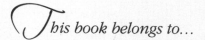 *This book belongs to...*

_____

*a woman who desires
to live a better life.*

GROWTH & STUDY GUIDE

Small Changes
for a Better
Life

Elizabeth George

HARVEST HOUSE PUBLISHERS

EUGENE, OREGON

Cover by Terry Dugan Design, Minneapolis, Minnesota

Cover photo © Dana Edmunds, Getty Images

Acknowledgment

As always, thank you to my dear husband, Jim George, M. Div., Th. M., for your able assistance, guidance, suggestions, and loving encouragement on this project.

SMALL CHANGES FOR A BETTER LIFE GROWTH AND STUDY GUIDE
Taken from *God's Wisdom for a Woman's Life*
Copyright © 2003 by Elizabeth George
Published by Harvest House Publishers
Eugene, Oregon 97402
www.harvesthousepublishers.com

ISBN-13: 978-0-7369-1784-1
ISBN-10: 0-7369-1784-5

Printed in the United States of America

06 07 08 09 10 /BP-KB/ 10 9 8 7 6 5 4 3 2 1

Contents

A Word of Welcome

Dear Reader...

As you hold this book in your hands and prepare to launch into this exciting growth and study guide designed to help set in motion the changes you desire, the changes that will help you live out God's plan for your life, please do these few things:

Open your book... and review each chapter in the book *Small Changes for a Better Life.*

Open "the Book," the Bible... and follow along through the scriptures in each lesson to see for yourself what God has to say about His plan and your life.

Open your eyes... to God's message to you personally about any changes that would be helpful or are needed. Remember, prayer is essential.

Open your heart... to any changes God prompts you to make. Look for His lessons from His heart to yours.

Open your heart...to others. If you want to study with others who are seeking a better life—a life that glorifies God by living out His plan—you can find information for "Leading a Bible Study Discussion Group" in the back of this study guide or on my website: www.ElizabethGeorge.com.

As you follow these few steps, you'll see God causing you to be "transformed by the renewing of your mind" and "conformed to the image of His Son" (Romans 12:2 and 8:29).

In His everlasing love,

Elizabeth George

Ask for Wisdom

 In your copy of *Small Changes for a Better Life* read the chapter titled "Small Change #1—Ask for Wisdom." What from this chapter meant the most to you, offered you the greatest challenge, or helped you make the changes necessary for a better life?

As you launch into this exciting study about the small changes you can make for a better life, take a minute to write a few sentences that describe your lifestyle and the kinds of decisions you must make on a regular basis.

Review the quotations at the beginning of this chapter in your book. Write here the one you like best and why.

"Lord, Give Me Wisdom"

Read the story about King Solomon from 1 Kings 3:4-15 in your Bible. Also read the corresponding account of Solomon's encounter with God in 2 Chronicles 1:6-13. From these accounts, in what ways do you witness Solomon following the guidelines for wisdom taught in these scriptures?

Proverbs 4:7—

Proverbs 4:11—

Proverbs 8:11—

James 1:5—

Now for you—How are you faring in following Solomon's example of actively pursuing, desiring, and asking for wisdom? Note any weak areas. Then write out what you will do to begin asking for wisdom on a more regular basis.

Daily Steps Toward a Better Life

Write out each of the four steps toward wisdom from your book and answer the questions regarding them.

Step 1—

Consider Solomon's situation again. Above what other things did he desire God's wisdom (see 1 Kings 3:11)?

Regarding long life: What did Solomon write regarding wisdom in...

...Proverbs 3:16?

...Proverbs 9:11?

Regarding wealth: What did Solomon write regarding the value of wisdom in...

...Proverbs 3:13-15?

Regarding triumph over enemies: According to Proverbs 16:7, why was seeking wisdom a good choice?

Step 2—

Again, recalling 1 Kings 3, how did Solomon model for us this step toward wisdom?

Look now at another great man and leader of God's people. How did Nehemiah also live out this most important step toward gaining wisdom in Nehemiah 1:4-6?

Step 3—

Look up and read Proverbs 2:1-6. What efforts must be made to obtain wisdom?

What does verse 6 have to say about where you are to seek wisdom?

Now look at Proverbs 8:17. What do you learn here about how hard you must seek wisdom?

Revisit James 1:5. Where did James say you are to seek wisdom?

Step 4—

As in every area of your life, you must also grow in wisdom. What are some keys to growing in wisdom according to...

...Proverbs 4:6?

...Proverbs 8:33?

...Proverbs 8:34?

Bonus blessing #1—For a glimpse at God's blessings upon King Solomon due to his request for wisdom above all other things, read 1 Kings 3:16-28 and 4:29-34. In a few words, how did God bless Solomon?

Bonus blessing #2—For an example and a glimpse of God's answer to Solomon's request for wisdom above all things, read 2 Chronicles 1:14-17. In a few words, how did God bless Solomon?

A Woman of Amazing Wisdom

Meet Abigail—Acquaint yourself with her splendid wisdom by scanning 1 Samuel 25:2-39. As you read, note here in a few words how Abigail exhibited...

...wisdom

...discretion

...faithfulness

What do you most admire about Abigail that you want to take away from this lesson and make true in your life?

Just for Today

A note of instruction—I will not be guiding you through this practical and personal section on the lessons to follow, but I do want to walk through a sample of how you can work the suggested exercises in the book *Small Changes for a Better Life*. The point is to do as much as you can to apply God's principles to your life. If you are completing these lessons on your own, your answers testify to your diligence, faithfulness, and sincerity in seeking out God's plan for you. They provide a record and mark your progress as you journey toward putting God's principles to work for you. If you are part of a group, write what you will share as you are accountable to others and encourage others.

Also consider purchasing a personal journal for logging your growth. This will encourage your heart and add yet another discipline to your life. As Donald Whitney writes in his book on spiritual health, an example of practicing personal discipline "is in the keeping of a spiritual journal."[1]

❧ *Just for today*…Share how you followed through on the assignment. (For instance, did you follow through? What chapter of Proverbs did you read? What verse did you choose to write on your card? Did you carry it with you? Did you use the wisdom, and if so, how?)

❧ *Just for tomorrow*…Share how you followed through on this assignment. (For instance, did you zero in on a decision to make? Did youu pray for wisdom? From whom did you or will you seek counsel?)

❧ *Just for this week*…Share how you followed through on this assignment. (For instance, what commentary on the book of Proverbs did you borrow, check out, purchase, or put on your shopping list? Did you read along with it each day when you read your chapter of Proverbs for the day?)

Living God's Plan

Read the "Living God's Plan" section in your book again. As you consider the contents of this chapter and "God's Guidelines for a Better Life," what principle or guideline really spoke to your heart...and what do you plan to do about it?

Order Your Life

In your copy of *Small Changes for a Better Life* read the chapter titled "Small Change #2—Order Your Life." What from this chapter meant the most to you, offered you the greatest challenge, or helped you make the small changes necessary for a better life?

As you step into this exciting lesson that focuses on a woman's priorities, think about your daily schedule and the flow of your week. Also take a look at your calendar for the past and present week. What do the facts reveal about the priorities you are living out on a daily basis? Where...and with whom...and on what...are you spending your time? Your energy?

Priority One—Put God First

1. This chapter began with praise for the woman pictured in Proverbs 31:10-31. What do you learn about her key to success in verse 30?

   What more do you learn from...

   ...Proverbs 10:27?

   ...Proverbs 14:26?

   ...Proverbs 14:27?

   ...Proverbs 19:23?

   ...Proverbs 29:25?

2. Do you realize the need for wisdom in managing your busy life? If so, where must you seek it according to...

   ...Psalm 19:7?

   ...Psalm 119:130?

3. How does the Word of God say we can and should "begin with God"?

   Matthew 6:33—

   Matthew 22:37—

   1 Corinthians 2:1-2—

Is there anything you need to do to act upon living according to this all-important first and ultimate priority? What first step will you take today?

Priority Two—Serve Others

Read Matthew 22:39. What is our attitude toward others to be?

How did Jesus say to live this out in Matthew 20:26?

And in Matthew 20:27?

How did Jesus serve others in Matthew 20:28?

Know God's order of priorities—If you are married, who (and what) does God's Word say are to be the priorities in your life as found in...

...Matthew 19:5?

...1 Corinthians 7:34?

...Titus 2:4?

...Proverbs 14:1 and 31:27?

If you are not married, what does God's Word say is to be the priority of your life as stated in...

...1 Corinthians 7:34?

Take a minute to share how your initial assessment of your priorities measures up to this list. Are you on track, or do you need to make some changes? Please explain.

Plan to practice God's priorities—Proverbs 16:1 centers on planning. Write it out here.

By preparations (or plans) Solomon meant the "placing of things in order" as in "setting a battle-array" or "laying a fire."[2] God, of course, has the final say in your life, which includes your day. It's wise and valuable to practice God's priorities. If this week didn't look so good when you completed the exercise at the beginning of this lesson, or if it revealed the fact that your priorities are out of whack, take calendar and planner in hand and place a few things in order. Set a battle-array for next week. Turn things around by planning to practice God's priorities. Check here when done_____. Then jot down what the following proverbs add to your concept of planning and its importance.

Proverbs 16:3—

Proverbs 16:9—

Eliminate nonessential activities—Are you perhaps failing to serve others because of any of the selfish habits that follow? Check any that need your undivided and immediate attention.

___laziness ___sleeping in ___lounging
___shopping ___running around ___telephone
___Internet ___TV ___hobbies

As you think back to planning and "placing things in order" and "setting a battle-array," what is your plan for eliminating excesses in these areas so you can better serve others? List at least three things you will do, change, or eliminate to follow God's priorities for a wise woman.

1.

2.

3.

Priority Three—Take Care of Yourself

Now, for yourself...and planning to practice God's priorities—Follow the exercises suggested in your book:

When will you get up?

When will you go to bed?

When will you eat?

What will you eat?

When will you exercise?

What will those exercises be?

When will you take your vitamins?

What other disciplines could you use in your life?

Write out your answers, schedule them into your planner at the designated times, and pray for God's help in following through. As an added step, write in a journal or keep some kind of record of the growth and changes God is prompting in you. Write out the differences you experience as you put these disciplines in place. Your transformation will be a testimony to God. For the sake of the battle, how do these verses fortify you in the discipline of your eating habits?

Proverbs 23:2—

Proverbs 30:8—

1 Corinthians 10:31—

Galatians 5:23—

Bonus blessing—We'll continue to look at God's example of a woman of wisdom in Proverbs 31:10-31, so take a couple of minutes to read through these 22 verses. Note her priorities and the disciplines that enabled her to practice them. How do you see her living out...

Priority #1—God?

Priority #2—Others?

Priority #3—Self?

Others praised her...and now it's your turn. What quality or practice do you most want to imitate from her wise life? And why?

Just for Today

❧ *Just for today...*

❧ *Just for tomorrow...*

❧ *Just for this week...*

Living God's Plan

Read the "Living God's Plan" section in your book again. As you consider the contents of this chapter and "God's Guidelines for a Better Life," what principle or guideline really spoke to your heart...and what do you plan to do about it?

Own Your Purpose

 In your copy of *Small Changes for a Better Life* read the chapter titled "Small Change #3—Own Your Purpose." What from this chapter meant the most to you, offered you the greatest challenge, or helped you make the small changes necessary for a better life?

Enjoy the Promise of Eternal Life

Every woman needs encouragement in performing her daily tasks and duties. How do these scriptures about eternal life encourage you in your work today?

Psalm 16:11—

2 Corinthians 4:17—

1 Peter 1:3-4—

1 John 3:2—

Note how you can know that you have eternal life according to these verses:

John 1:12—

John 3:16—

John 6:47—

Romans 6:23—

1 John 5:11-12—

1 John 5:13—

In your book you were asked, "Do you possess the hope of eternal life?" How did you answer this most important question? Write a few sentences from your heart about your "hope of eternal life."

Are you sure of eternal life? If so, pray and thank God pro-fusely.

Are you uncertain? If so, consider the following prayers regarding your faith in God's Word and in God's Son, Jesus Christ.

> Jesus, I know I am a sinner, but I want to repent of my sins and turn and follow You. I believe that You died for my sins and rose again victorious over the power of sin and death, and I want to accept You as my personal Savior. Come into my life, Lord Jesus, and help me obey You from this day forward.

> Jesus, I know that in the past I asked You into my life. I thought at that time that I was Your child, but my life hasn't shown the fruit of my belief. As I again hear Your call, I want to make a real commitment to You as the Lord and Master of my life.

> Jesus, I know that in the past I asked You into my life. I want to be Your child, I think and hope that I am your child, but I want to know that I am Your child. Lord, give me the reassurance that I have eternal life through You because of Your death on the cross for my sin (1 John 5:13).

Now, which was the prayer of your heart, and why?

Grow in Your Spiritual Life

Check out these scriptures in your Bible. How do they challenge you as you face your day...and your life...and faithfully live out God's plan and purpose for you?

Romans 8:29—

Romans 12:2—

2 Corinthians 4:16—

As you look at Hebrews 5:12, could these words have been written to and of you about your spiritual life? Please explain why or why not.

Continuing on with the challenge to nurture your spiritual life, how do these scriptures motivate you to pursue spiritual growth?

Matthew 4:4—

1 Corinthians 14:20—

Ephesians 4:14—

Ephesians 5:17—

2 Timothy 3:16-17—

Hebrews 5:12-14—

1 Peter 2:2—

2 Peter 3:18—

What consistent resource did you observe regarding how spiritual growth occurs?

Consider again the challenges of life…and particularly your life. What are three steps you can take on a regular basis to ensure your spiritual growth?

1.

2.

3.

What do these truths have to say regarding the strength to do what you purpose to do?

Nehemiah 8:10—

Psalm 27:1 and 29:11—

Isaiah 40:31—

Philippians 4:13—

Think again about your God-ordained purposes in life and what it takes to faithfully live them out. How does a vibrant spiritual life help?

Get a Handle on Your Practical Life

In a few sentences, describe your practical life in terms of...

> *Family life*—(For instance, who are the people at home that make up your day, and what challenges do they present?)

> *Others*—(Besides family, whose lives do you touch most often? In the neighborhood, at work, at school? Are you available to them? Are you actively involved in ministry to them?)

Physical life and health—(What physical demands are placed on you each day? And how is your health? Are you up for the challenge?)

Ministry life—(Again, besides family, who are those you serve, help, give to, or talk to about Jesus?)

Manage Your Daily Life

Think about it...do you tend to live for the future, putting things off, taking it easy, waiting until...(whatever!)? Or are you a "today" woman, giving your all today and refusing to eat "the bread of idleness" (Proverbs 31:27)? Are you striving to accomplish as much as you can for God, family, and others in your 1,440 minutes each day? How do the following scriptures educate you, convict you, and motivate you regarding your daily life?

Luke 12:16-21—

James 4:13-15—

Read these verses in your Bible and after each one list at least one way to turn up the heat of your heart so that yours is...

...a godly walk—Micah 6:8

...a passionate walk—Philippians 3:13-14

...a sober walk—Ephesians 5:15-16

...a wise walk—Ephesians 5:17

Just for Today

Jonathan Edwards made five resolutions in his youth. Number One on his list was: "Live with all my might while I do live."

Number Two on his list was: "Never lose one moment of time, but improve it in the most profitable way possible." (He died at 55.)

❧ *Just for today...*

❧ *Just for tomorrow...*

❧ *Just for this week...*

Living God's Plan

Read the "Living God's Plan" section in your book again. As you consider the contents of this chapter and "God's Guidelines for a Better Life," what principle or guideline really spoke to your heart...and what do you plan to do about it?

Read Your Bible

In your copy of *Small Changes for a Better Life* read the chapter titled "Small Change #4— Read Your Bible." What from this chapter meant the most to you, offered you the greatest challenge, or helped you make the small changes necessary for a better life?

The Three Stages of Bible Reading

Before you begin this all-important lesson about God's Word, the Bible, look again at the three stages of Bible reading. Write out which stage best describes you and tell why.

The Treasure of God's Word

This study is about small changes for a better life. And where is the wisdom for that better life to be found? In the treasure of God's Word, the Bible! As one Bible teacher explains, "Before you try to obtain an object it is best to determine its source or where it can be found. If you desire food, you go to the grocery store where it is sold. If you want clothing, you go to the retailer who handles this type of merchandise. When it comes to wisdom for a better life, the Bible makes it very clear where the source is to be found. It is in God."[3]

Copy Proverbs 2:6 here from your Bible. Then read the explanatory words from several respected Bible commentators shared below.

> God is the fountain of all knowledge… "Wisdom," "knowledge," and "understanding"…comes, as it were, from his mouth to our ears.[4]

> The wisdom of the Word brings us into a kind of life we never knew before. We find that the Lord is in the habit of providing wisdom, for He is its source [Proverbs 2:6]. From God's mouth comes His Word, which gives us an intimate knowledge of Him as well as understanding, or discrimination in judgment.[5]

As you assess the importance and the power of the treasure of God's Word, consider these two scenarios.

How did Jesus reprimand the religious group called the Sadducees in Matthew 22:29?

How is it that Daniel was able to interpret Nebuchadnezzar's dream according to Daniel 2:19-23?

Now look at Proverbs 2, verse 4. How strenuously does this scripture say you are to look for the treasure of God's Word? In your own words, describe how tough this might be.

Recount now your last venture into the mine of God's Word in terms of time, energy, and passion. Did your efforts measure up to the challenge in Proverbs 2:4? Please explain your answer.

The Bible comes from God—You've looked at 2 Timothy 3:16 before, but read it again. What does this verse teach about the Bible?

And 2 Peter 1:21?

Now ponder this information:

> God is wisdom. God has wisdom. God is ready and
> willing to give you that wisdom for a better life if
> you will meet the conditions He has laid out in His
> Word. Out of His mouth, through the writings of
> holy men of God moved by the Holy Spirit, He has
> given us His Word. That is the revelation of His
> knowledge and understanding. Beyond the shadow
> of a doubt, the greatest gift ever bestowed on the
> human race—apart from the salvation wrought by
> Jesus Christ, the living Word—is the Holy Bible, the
> written Word.[6]

Do you agree? And if so, explain how important this makes
the habit of seeking out the treasure of God's Word and why.

The Bible causes you to grow in Christlikeness—Read
2 Corinthians 3:18. What is its message to your heart?

What do these scriptures teach you about how applying
God's Word causes you to grow in Christlikeness?

Romans 12:2—

Ephesians 4:22-24—

2 Timothy 3:14-15—

The apostle Paul desired that his beloved friends in Ephesus
would "grow up" in Christ. Read his exhortation for yourself
in Ephesians 4:14-15. Are you praying this for yourself? What
must you do to make Paul's desire yours as well?

Unearthing the Treasure of God's Wisdom

Now that you know and acknowledge that God's Word is treasure, how can you go about the business of unearthing that treasure?

Step 1: Read it—What example or wise advice do these people of the Bible have to pass on regarding the importance of reading God's Word, the Bible?

Moses in Exodus 24:7—

The king in Deuteronomy 17:19-20—

Joshua in Joshua 8:34-35—

Ezra in Nehemiah 8:1-3—

Isaiah in Isaiah 34:16—

Step 2: Study it—What example or wise advice do these people of the Bible have to pass on regarding the importance of studying God's Word, the Bible?

Jesus in John 5:39—

The Bereans in Acts 17:11—

Step 3: Hear it—From what wise and gifted people can you hear the Word of God...and where?

Ephesians 4:11-12—

Titus 2:3—

Hebrews 10:24-25—

Step 4: Memorize it—How can God's Word hidden in your heart benefit your life?

    Joshua 1:8—

    Psalm 1:2-3—

    Psalm 37:31—

    Psalm 119:11—

    Proverbs 2:1-2—

Step 5: Devour it—"To delight" means to take pleasure in and to enjoy. How did these saints devour God's Word, and what were its wondrous effects?

    Job 23:12—

    Jeremiah 15:16—

In your own words, summarize the significance of reading, studying, hearing, memorizing, and devouring the Bible. Then note your plan for making the treasure of God's wisdom and instruction yours.

Just for Today

"Open the book of God and read a portion there; that it may hallow all thy thoughts, and sweeten all thy care."[7]

❦ *Just for today...*

❦ *Just for tomorrow...*

❧ *Just for this week...*

Living God's Plan

Read the "Living God's Plan" section in your book again. As you consider the contents of this chapter and "God's Guidelines for a Better Life," what principle or guideline really spoke to your heart...and what do you plan to do about it?

Develop Your Prayer Life

In your copy of *Small Changes for a Better Life* read the chapter titled "Small Change #5— Develop Your Prayer Life." What from this chapter meant the most to you, offered you the greatest challenge, or helped you make the small changes necessary for a better life?

Before you head into the why's and how's of developing a prayer life, let's take your heart's temperature. It always helps to know what you are dealing with before you embark on bettering your life.

Describe the last time you spent time alone in prayer (not with your husband, friend, Bible-study members, Sunday school class, Christian workmates, or mothers' group). When (as in the date) was it, and what time of day was it? And where were you? About how long was your prayer time? Did you use any tools—your Bible, a prayer journal, prayer guide, or hymn book?

Talk to God

Discipline is training that develops self-control, character, orderliness, or efficiency. I'm sure that's what you want when it comes to your prayer life. And as with any discipline, a dynamic prayer life must be carefully cultivated and developed. Look now at the kinds of efforts you can make in this vital area of prayer.

Do it!—How did David say to go about "doing it" when it came to the when of prayer (Psalm 5:3)?

And in Psalm 55:17?

How did Jesus say to go about "doing it" when it came to the where of prayer (Matthew 6:6)?

Do it badly—What did Jesus say about the "wrong" way to pray in Matthew 6:5 and 7?

Rather than being interested in a formula and eloquence in prayer, what was Jesus looking for instead according to Luke 18:9-14?

What truths can you make your own regarding "doing it" and "doing it badly" after reading the passages on prayer? List three.

1.

2.

3.

Do it regularly—Look again at Psalm 55:17 and compare it with 1 Thessalonians 5:17. What is the message?

Hebrews 4:15-16—What is the message here?

Psalm 92:1-2—Regarding these words, someone has written, "Prayer is the key of the morning and the bolt of the night." How do these verses encourage regular prayer?

Do it faithfully—The statement was made in your book that prayer helps you keep a clean slate with God. How do these scriptures encourage your faithfulness in confessing your sins in prayer?

Psalm 66:18—

1 John 1:9—

Psalm 32:5—

Do it for life—In all things Jesus is the perfect model. To the very end, what was His habit according to Luke 23:46 and 1 Peter 2:23?

Follow Jesus' Model Prayer

What was the disciples' earnest plea to their Lord in Luke 11:1?

How did Jesus answer them in Luke 11:2-4?

Prayer is personal—What phrase from the Lord's Prayer teaches you this aspect about prayer?

According to these verses, what is the tender relationship Christians enjoy with God?

Matthew 6:4,6, and 8—

Matthew 7:11—

Galatians 4:6—

Prayer acknowledges God's authority—What phrase from the Lord's Prayer teaches you this aspect about prayer?

What further information regarding God's rule do you learn from Revelation 19:16?

Prayer acknowledges your trust—What phrase from the Lord's Prayer teaches you this aspect about prayer?

How did Jesus demonstrate His trust in Matthew 26:42?

Prayer indicates your dependence—What phrase from the Lord's Prayer teaches you this aspect about prayer?

How do these verses increase your awareness of your dependence upon God?

Psalm 23:1—

Psalm 37:25—

Matthew 6:25—

1 Timothy 6:8—

Prayer entreats God's guidance—What phrase from the Lord's Prayer teaches you this aspect about prayer?

How do these verses increase your understanding of God's guidance?

Psalm 23:2-3—

Psalm 32:8—

Psalm 121:8—

Proverbs 15:19—

James 1:5—

Following the Path of Discipline

Remember the definition of "discipline" given earlier in this lesson? "Discipline is training that develops self-control, character, orderliness, or efficiency." How do we go about developing the spiritual discipline of prayer? Consider this insight regarding nurturing discipline from my book *Life Management for Busy Women*:

> Like in every woman's life, there are days when praying is your heart's delight. And there are days, too, when you do it because it is the right thing to do...and you know it...and it requires determination and a decision to do it. Beloved, that's the way it is with a discipline—any discipline. You do it because it is what you need to do and are supposed to do and because it is the right thing to do. You do it because it contributes to and propels you toward what you want to be and do. And then...somehow...the duty of the discipline turns into sheer delight, and you reap the blessings of a priceless, tender relationship with the Lord a thousandfold.[8]

Note where you are at present in your quest for the hard-won discipline of regular prayer. Then write out a "Prayer of Commitment" regarding following the path of greater discipline in your prayer life.

Just for Today

The more you pray, the easier it becomes. The easier it becomes, the more you will pray.

❧ *Just for today...*

❧ *Just for tomorrow...*

❧ *Just for this week...*

Living God's Plan

Read the "Living God's Plan" section in your book again. As you consider the contents of this chapter and "God's Guidelines for a Better Life," what principle or guideline really spoke to your heart...and what do you plan to do about it?

Pursue Spiritual Growth

In your copy of *Small Changes for a Better Life* read the chapter titled "Small Change #6—Pursue Spiritual Growth." What from this chapter meant the most to you, offered you the greatest challenge, or helped you make the small changes necessary for a better life?

A Sure Formula for Growth

Walk through this chapter by first writing each step for pursuing spiritual growth after its letter in the word G-R-O-W-T-H. Then answer the questions concerning each step.

G—

God's will is that you grow spiritually. How do these verses bear out this statement?

Ephesians 4:14-15—

2 Thessalonians 1:3—

1 Peter 2:2—

2 Peter 3:18—

Look up these scriptures and note where spiritual life and spiritual growth begin.

Proverbs 9:10—

John 11:25—

Now take a walk down what is called "The Romans Road," noting what each verse teaches about your spiritual life.

Romans 3:23—

Romans 5:8—

Romans 6:23—

Romans 10:9-10—

After this little "walk," do you consider yourself to be walking with Jesus Christ? Please explain your answer. If not, please look again at the prayers on page 27. Which one suits the need of your heart?

R—

It's good to know what God's Word, the Bible, has to say about sin. What do you learn in these verses?

Romans 3:23—

Romans 5:12—

1 John 1:8—

Once again, look at 1 Peter 2:1-2. How must sin be handled so that spiritual growth may occur? (It helps to know that to "lay aside" means to put off as one puts off and lays aside a garment. Like you would strip off a soiled garment, so you must rid yourself of evil. As one scholarly source explains it, "There is a negative and purging phase in holiness."[9])

Revisit 1 John 1:9. What is its message regarding sin?

Proverbs offers another help toward gaining wisdom in this area of sin. What does Proverbs 28:13 say it is?

O—

Second Peter 1:5-8 details the plan of spiritual growth. You could call it the "add to" passage of Scripture. Read it now. What is this divine plan for growth? Answer by listing the seven add-ons of faith.

>   __   __

>   __   __

>   __   __

>   __

According to verse 8, what is the result of such diligent attention to spiritual growth?

We grow by the Word of God. What kind of appetite for God and His Word did these writers experience and express?

>   Psalm 42:1-2—

>   Psalm 63:1—

>   Psalm 84:2—

>   Matthew 5:6—

How can such cravings be fulfilled according to John 7:37?

Describe your present appetite for God's Word in a few sentences. How does your desire to grow measure up to that of the writers of the scriptures just mentioned?

W—

As an often-heard saying reminds us about all growth, you are either moving forward or backward; there is no such thing as standing still. What do these scriptures teach us about the ways and means of spiritual growth? (Be sure to note the verbs, the active part of each sentence.)

> 1 Corinthians 9:24—
>
> Philippians 3:13-14—
>
> 2 Timothy 4:7—
>
> Hebrews 12:1—

This step is called "W—Work out a method and rate for growth." Look again at the possibilities listed in your book. Then decide what you will do and set your personal goals to match up with the desires of your heart. For instance, some women set a goal to do one thing each month to grow, such as listen through a series of teaching tapes, attend a Bible seminar or workshop, join a Bible study, enroll in a Bible class, or read a helpful or "meaty" book. What will it to be for you?

T—

We all need help with spiritual growth...and God is faithful
to provide it.

Who in the body of Christ is to help and teach the younger
women in the church, according to Titus 2:3?

What kind of woman is she to be (also verse 3)?

-

-

-

What is she to teach in a discipling relationship?

Verse 4: —

—

Verse 5: —

—

—

Who do you consider to be your "older women"?

Who do you consider to be your "younger women"?

Are any changes called for? Please explain.

H—

On a reading through the book of Psalms, I kept a record in my personal journal of every utterance of the two words "I will" that tumbled out of the heart and rolled off the pen of the individual psalmists. When I was done, I was well acquainted with the need for and the power of decisiveness. Note the spiritual discipline spoken of in just these few "I wills," and don't be surprised if they are familiar.

Psalm 5:3—

Psalm 119:8—

Psalm 55:17—

Psalm 119:16—

Psalm 63:1—

What decisions will you make to maintain your spiritual growth? Note them here. (And P.S.—Begin each one with the words "I will.")

Just for Today

❧ *Just for today...*

❧ *Just for tomorrow...*

❧ *Just for this week...*

Living God's Plan

Read the "Living God's Plan" section in your book again. As you consider the contents of this chapter and "God's Guidelines for a Better Life," what principle or guideline really spoke to your heart...and what do you plan to do about it?

Manage Your Life

In your copy of *Small Changes for a Better Life* read the chapter titled "Small Change #7— Manage Your Life." What from this chapter meant the most to you, offered you the greatest challenge, or helped you make the small changes necessary for a better life?

Step 1: Own the Management of Your Life

Managing your life begins with knowing what things are important to you and learning how to prioritize them. The dictionary defines the word "prioritize" as...

>...precedence in time, order, and importance,

>...to arrange items in order of priority, and

>...to assign an item to a particular level of priority.

Begin the better management of your life by making a list of
God's priorities for a wise woman according to Titus 2:3-5.
If this passage is beginning to look familiar, "Bravo!" It's a
key text for God's plan for your life as a Christian woman.

When thinking of making improvements, it helps me to
think of the maxim, "A problem defined is a problem half
solved." At first glance, as you look at your own life laid
beside God's priority list, do you see any areas where your
attention is lacking? What are they?

Step 2: Prioritize Your Time

Your book dealt with priority uses of time. Consider each
one of them now. And as you do, remember the definition
of "priority" and prioritize.

> *Time with God*—How does Matthew 6:33 encourage
> you to make God and time with God your first pri-
> ority...and what does it say about the other areas,
> issues, concerns, and duties of your life? Answer and
> then revisit the quotation regarding time found at the
> beginning of this chapter in your book: The last line of
> the quote says it all. "Take time for God—it is life's
> only lasting investment."

Time with your husband—If you are married, think back over this past week. How many minutes have you and your husband been alone together? And if the minutes were few, why? What were the culprits?

What one thing can you do to improve in this important priority area and give it more time this week?

Time with your children—If you have children, evaluate the time you spent with each child this past week.

Susanna Wesley, the mother of John and Charles Wesley (and 17 other children—several of whom died before the age of two), spent one hour per week alone with each child. What simple steps can you take to increase your time with each child? And while you're doing this exercise, keep in mind that the best thing a mother can spend on her children is time—not money.

Time with family and friends—Hear this penetrating thought (or is it meant to be a joke?): "Isn't it aggravating how little value other people put on your time?" Again, evaluate the amount of time you are spending with family and friends. How does this time compare with the time you are spending with your husband and children? Are your husband and children receiving the bulk and the best of your time in comparison to others? Is some reassignment of time needed?

Time for yourself—With your busy schedule, time is limited. Where in your day could you find 15 minutes to be alone to recharge your batteries? And what would you do in that 15 minutes? (Be sure to look at the quotation at the front of this chapter in your book. The words that caught my eye were "Take time to think—it is the source of power. Take time to read— it is the fountain of wisdom." What caught your eye?)

Time for the unexpected—Henry Kissinger, while he served as Secretary of State, said, "There can't be a crisis next week. There's no time in my schedule!"[10] It's funny, isn't it, how we think we are in control of our schedules? But reality teaches us differently. Plan as we may, our plans may be—and probably will be— interrupted, changed, altered, and many times thrown out altogether. How are you when it comes to handling the unexpected? And what is your attitude when changes emerge?

Behold now the Master—See how Jesus handled
an "interruption" to His plan to withdraw and
pray after learning of John the Baptist's death.
First, what was the interruption and how did
Jesus respond in Matthew 14:13-14? Then note
how this episode ended in verses 22 and 23.

Make note of several lessons you can learn from
the Master about graciously managing interrup-
tions. Then take them with you into your next
day.

Time for planning—It's been said, "Either you plan
your day, or someone else will be glad to plan it for
you." And "God has a wonderful plan for your life,
and so does everyone else!" It's also been recom-
mended that you spend at least five minutes each
morning planning your day before you begin it. I personally plan at least 15 minutes each morning and 30
minutes several times during each week. Now I ask
you, where in your day can you set aside a few minutes to plan? (And don't forget, a good time to think
about this is the night before.)

Do you need to purchase a yearly planner or a
planner pad that allows you to tear off each day,
week, and month? Or can you print one off the
Internet? What other tools could help you become
a better and wiser planner?

Time for work—What standard items do you need to carry with you each day to your workplace or school or on your errands? Take time to think through your days and make an all-inclusive list. Then consider how your revealing answers to this one question can free your time up each morning as you prepare for your work. And how much preparation can you do the night before?

As every thread of gold is valuable, so is every moment of your time. That's why prioritizing your time is essential to gaining wisdom. The psalmist prayed to gain a heart of wisdom. How was he planning to move toward such a cherished prize? By numbering his days (Psalm 90:12). The apostle Paul prayed to redeem time. And how was he planning to do that? By walking carefully and wisely and by watching over his minutes (Colossians 4:5). What is the prayer of your heart regarding planning, prioritizing, and practicing your priorities so that you have time with God, with loved ones, for yourself, for others, and for your work?

Step 3: Learn What's Important

Briefly, as we end this lesson, how can you:

> *Learn to be more effective*—Based on the priorities addressed in this lesson, do you consider yourself to be efficient or effective...or both or neither? Please explain.

> *Learn to eliminate*—What is your answer to the question, What can be eliminated from my life at this time that is not a priority?

Just for Today

🌿 *Just for today...*

✻ *Just for tomorrow...*

✻ *Just for this week...*

Living God's Plan

Read the "Living God's Plan" section in your book again. As you consider the contents of this chapter and "God's Guidelines for a Better Life," what principle or guideline really spoke to your heart...and what do you plan to do about it?

Live by a Schedule

In your copy of *Small Changes for a Better Life* read the chapter titled "Small Change #8—Live by a Schedule." What from this chapter meant the most to you, offered you the greatest challenge, or helped you make the small changes necessary for a better life?

In chapter 8 in your book you read about how my friend Julie changed my life with a few wise words. God also gave me another life-changing friend who at one time studied under the famous Peter Drucker, prominent management authority and the "father of effective management." This woman had much to teach me about time and life management, about planning, scheduling, and executing mountains of work. Her mentor, Dr. Drucker, said, "Nothing so much distinguishes effective executives as their tender loving care of time....Those executives who really get things done don't start with their work: they start with their time."[11]

You too are an executive, a CEO, head of operations, a manager. Think about it. You are entrusted by God to manage not only your own life but the lives of those you live with. You are also to oversee your productivity, your body, your spiritual growth, your service to God, your schoolwork, your work...and the list of management responsibilities goes on. Plus you've been given the oversight of the most important institution in the world—a home.

Are you catching the vision? You are to be an "effective executive." You are to be distinguished by your "tender loving care of time." You are to get things done by starting with the scheduling of your time...so that the work gets accomplished. So you must roll up your "executive shirtsleeves," put on your thinking cap, hang a "Manager" sign on your door, and master the fine art of scheduling.

"A List of Projected Operations"

What is a schedule?—Copy out of your book the dictionary definition of "schedule" here.

Now think about your "projected operations" for this week. Based on what you are learning in your book, what are they? What do you wish to accomplish...and what must you accomplish?

Solomon, the wisest person who ever lived before Christ, made a schedule. What is one "operation" he came up with on his "projected operations" list in 1 Kings 4:7? And what can you learn about scheduling from Solomon's wise solution?

Why have a schedule?—Note these three reasons.

1. *God's purpose*—See Acts 27:22-25. The apostle Paul considered himself to belong to God. And he considered serving God and worshiping God to be his purpose in life. How do the following scriptures help you relate to Paul's passionate perception of his life and God's purpose?

    Ephesians 1:11—

    Colossians 1:16—

    Romans 8:28—

    2 Timothy 1:9—

As you go about your daily business and the operations of your life, how much do you think about and plan around God's purpose for your life? For your day? For your work? Put your answers down in minutes. As you review your calculations, what adjustments are called for?

2. *Your manner*—Several proverbs point to the poor results, emotions, and chaos that can permeate a day with no plan. In a few words, note each proverb's message.

> Proverbs 13:4a—
>
> Proverbs 15:19a—
>
> Proverbs 19:2b—
>
> Proverbs 19:15—
>
> Proverbs 20:4—
>
> Proverbs 20:13a—
>
> Proverbs 21:5—
>
> Proverbs 24:30-31—

Recall a day when you actually created and followed a fairly good schedule. How was your emotional state during the day? At the end of that day? And was a decent amount of work accomplished? Take a few minutes to write out your recollections.

Look up the specific verses referred to in Proverbs 31. What do these teach you about the priorities of an ordered woman?

Proverbs 31:30—

Proverbs 31:13-15—

Proverbs 31:27—

Proverbs 31:20—

What do these teach about her schedule?

Proverbs 31:15—

Proverbs 31:27—

Proverbs 31:18—

Every woman needs a guide, a model, a mentor, or an example. Here in Proverbs 31 God gives you one. What lessons will you take away from her life?

Creating an Arrangement

In *Small Changes for a Better Life* you read about creating beautiful floral arrangements by positioning the flowers properly. In a similar way, we need to position certain parts of our schedule properly. Read Ecclesiastes 3:1-9. King Solomon speaks of the predictable "operations" in life. He observes that our lives run on a schedule, by routine, or in a cycle. They have a set scheme and appointed times. Read this list of daily "times."

The Daily Times

There is a time to get up...and a time to go to bed. There is a time to work...and a time to rest.

There is a time to seek God...and a time to serve God. There is a time to set up...and a time to act.

There is a time to prepare...and a time to execute. There is a time to plan...and a time to carry out those plans. There is a time to pray...and a time to move out.

There is a time to produce...and a time to play.

There is a time to care for others...and a time to be cared for by others. There is a time to live for Christ...and a time to die as gain.

What does your set scheme of things, your schedule, look like? Are you creating an arrangement by organizing the events of your life in some sort of schedule or are you merely allowing life to happen to you? Share your observations of your "Daily Times" here.

Creating a Schedule

It's time to create your schedule for just one day. Follow these steps and check when done.

Step 1—God. Write down a time when you will meet with God. Place that first on your fresh, blank schedule. _____

Step 2—People. Who are the people in your life? What will you do for them, and when? Transfer this information to your schedule. _____

Step 3—Future events. Make a list of your future events. Place them on your calendar. Then write down what you can do today in preparation for these future events. Write these activities on your schedule. _____

Step 4—Yourself. What will or must you do for yourself? Again make notes and schedule in yourself, even if only a five-minute slot is open. _____

Step 5—You'll surely be graduating to weekly, monthly, and yearly scheduling soon. Then you'll witness your "projected operations" lovingly and carefully tended to day by day blossom into a bold and beautiful future that produces a better life and honors the Lord.

Just for Today

❧ *Just for today...*

❧ *Just for tomorrow...*

❧ *Just for this week...*

Living God's Plan

Read the "Living God's Plan" section in your book again. As you consider the contents of this chapter and "God's Guidelines for a Better Life," what principle or guideline really spoke to your heart...and what do you plan to do about it?

Care for Your Home

In your copy of *Small Changes for a Better Life* read the chapter titled "Small Change #9—Care for Your Home." What from this chapter meant the most to you, offered you the greatest challenge, or helped you make the small changes necessary for a better life?

I paid a small tribute to my dear mother. Indeed, I never say, hear, or read the word "home" without thinking of her. Think now of your mother. What are some lessons on home that she instilled in you? Recall your meals, your holidays, her dishes, even her pots and pans. Picture her in her kitchen (even if it was only to make a cup of tea). Remember her favorite recipes—the "dishes" she's famous for. And remember her hobbies, too—what she loved to do. Not every woman has 100 percent fond memories of her mother. But there is surely something you can put your finger on that your mom imparted to you and blessed you with in the Home Department. And after you've done the remembering (and perhaps a little sniffling, too), if she's still living, write her a card or a letter and express your appreciation. I guarantee she'll save it!

A Home Must Be Built

> A house is built of logs and stones, of tiles and posts
> and tiers; a home is built of loving deeds that stand
> a thousand years.[12]

As we focus on "building" a home and "home building,"
look up these key verses in your favorite Bible and make
note of God's message through them to your heart.

Proverbs 9:1—

Proverbs 14:1—

Proverbs 24:3-4—

Proverbs 31:27—

Prayer—Every woman needs help with her homemaking.
And there's no doubt that prayer is Help with a capital H!
How do these verses encourage you to pray about your
home, a "daily" item on your must-do list?

Ephesians 5:20—

Philippians 4:6-7—

1 Thessalonians 5:17—

1 Thessalonians 5:18—

Prayer lifts homemaking out of the physical sphere and transports it into the spiritual realm. Have you tried it? If so, what did you discover? If not, try it...and then share what difference praying about your home, your homemaking, and the people in your home made in your attitude and efforts.

Resolution—How do these powerful and instructive scriptures help you in the Resolution Department?

Ecclesiastes 9:10—

Romans 12:11—

Philippians 3:13-14—

Colossians 3:17—

Colossians 3:23—

Here's how I got started down this path of resolve—I wrote out the following "I wills."

The Heart of a Homemaker

1. I will get up before my family in order to prepare myself spiritually and physically.

2. I will prepare breakfast for my family and sit with them while they eat.

3. I will work diligently to send every member of my family off in a good mood.

4. I will consult my husband every day to see if there is anything special he wants me to do for him.

5. I will keep a neat and orderly home.

6. I will respond positively.

7. I will personally meet and greet each family member as he or she returns home.

8. I will prepare special, good food for my family.

9. I will make dinner a special time.

10. I will grow daily in the areas of the Lord, marriage, family, and homemaking.[13]

Take time to write your own set of ten homemaking "I wills." Write them down...and don't forget to begin each one with the words "I will."

1.

2.

3.

4.

5.

6.

7.

8.

9.

10.

Presence—One of my maxims for life is "Nothing grand just happens," and that includes a home. Your time is limited. Plus you have a multitude of responsibilities. And you wear a variety of hats. However you simply must be there—be present—when your family is there. List three things you can give up in order to be present at home more often.

—

—

—

Next list three things you can give up while you are at home (television? telephone? hobbies?) that are robbing you of time and energy for your homemaking.

—

—

—

Time—How do you think one extra hour at home each day—or one extra hour of actual work while you are at home each day—will generate or create many wonderful "home improvements"?

Notice now how time was spent—and misspent—in these passages from Proverbs, the book of Wisdom.

Proverbs 6:6-11—

Proverbs 24:30-34—

A Home Is Built with Care

We've considered some positive elements that go into building a home. Look now at some home wreckers. Read each scripture in your Bible, and then note the behavior that is a detriment to a woman's desire to fulfill God's assignment to build a home.

Proverbs 14:1—

How do you think this is done, and how do you think it is a detriment?

Proverbs 31:27—

How do you think this is a detriment?

Just for Today

❧ Just for today...

❧ Just for tomorrow...

❧ Just for this week...

Living God's Plan

Read the "Living God's Plan" section in your book again. As you consider the contents of this chapter and "God's Guidelines for a Better Life," what principle or guideline really spoke to your heart...and what do you plan to do about it?

Invest in Your
Marriage

 In your copy of *Small Changes for a Better Life* read the chapter titled "Small Change #10— Invest in Your Marriage." What from this chapter meant the most to you, offered you the greatest challenge, or helped you make the small changes necessary for a better life?

Ten Keys to a Better Marriage

1. *Work as a team*—What does Genesis 2:18 say about God's idea of teamwork?

In the following scriptures, how does the wife contribute to the teamwork of her marriage?

Proverbs 31:12 and 31—

Acts 18:1-3—

Name one key way you could become a better "team player" with your husband. (And remember, it never hurts to ask him.)

2. Learn to communicate—Write out these verses on communication. Which ones should you commit to memory, and how will you apply them to yourself?

Proverbs 10:19—

Proverbs 15:1—

Proverbs 16:21—

James 1:19—

3. *Enjoy intimacy*—In your Bible, look up these whys and hows of sexual intimacy. How does each truth help your understanding of the importance and beauty of the physical aspect of a marriage relationship?

> *Proclaimed*—Genesis 2:24-25—
>
> *Procreation*—Genesis 1:27-28—
>
> *Pleasure*—Proverbs 5:15-19—
>
> *Purity*—1 Corinthians 7:2;—
> Hebrews 13:4—
>
> *Partnership*—1 Corinthians 7:3-4—
>
> *Protection*—1 Corinthians 7:5—

Intimacy in marriage is a wonderful gift from God. But like all good things, it doesn't just happen. Intimacy takes time and effort. What one thing can you do to create new opportunities?

4. *Manage your money*—Due to your position and role in the family, you are often, if not daily, put in the position of managing all or part of the family finances. You are a steward—one placed in a position of responsibility. First Corinthians 4:2 says a steward is to be found faithful or trustworthy. How would you describe your money management and stewardship up to this point? What one thing can you do to improve in this vital area of your marriage? What do you and your husband need to discuss regarding finances?

5. *Keep up the home*—You as a wife provide a ministry to those who dwell within your home-sweet-home when you keep up the home. How would you rate yourself as a home-lover and home-keeper (Titus 2:5)? How do you think your husband would rate you? What one major change must be made?

6. *Raise your children*—By working as a team, you and your husband provide consistency in discipline and structure for the family. What colossal error did Isaac and Rebekah make in raising Jacob and Esau (Genesis 25:28)?

Effective child-raising involves both parents. What are a few simple instructions found in Ephesians 6:4? (Note: The word "fathers" also has the meaning of "parents.")

And in Proverbs 22:6?

7. *Make time for fun*—Describe the last time you and your husband had fun together. Now plan for the next time.

Just for "fun," what activities did the happy couple in Song of Solomon 7:11-12 enjoy?

8. *Serve the Lord*—You already looked at Priscilla and Aquila as they worked together as a team (see Principle 1, Acts 18:1-3). Now describe this couple's service to the Lord and His people as shown in Romans 16:3-5.

What can you and your husband do together to serve the Lord? (For instance, can you open your home for a Bible study, serve at the next social, host a missionary overnight, give more of your money?) List some possibilities here and pray for a time to share them with your husband.

9. *Reach out to others*—Look again at Priscilla and Aquila as they reached out to another person in Acts 18:24-26. Who, why, and how did they reach out...and what was the result (verses 27-28)?

What is said about hospitality in...

   ...Romans 12:9,13?

   ...Titus 1:7-8?

   ...1 Peter 4:9?

What are some times and events when you and your husband can plan, as a team, to open your home and reach out to those in your neighborhood?

In your church?

From your workplace?

10. *Grow in the Lord*—In your book this principle appears in the "Living God's Plan" section. How do you think your faithful nurturing of your spiritual growth makes a difference in your relationship with your husband?

As you think about your growth in the Lord, how can you turn it up a notch? List three growth exercises you will put into place.

—

—

—

Just for Today

❧ *Just for today...*

❧ *Just for tomorrow...*

❧ *Just for this week...*

Living God's Plan

Read the "Living God's Plan" section in your book again. As you consider the contents of this chapter and "God's Guidelines for a Better Life," what principle or guideline really spoke to your heart...and what do you plan to do about it?

Train Your Children

In your copy of *Small Changes for a Better Life* read the chapter titled "Small Change #11— Train Your Children." What from this chapter meant the most to you, offered you the greatest challenge, or helped you make the small changes necessary for a better life?

Wisdom from a Godly Mother

1. As a mom, make a list of those who assist you regularly with your child-raising quandaries and questions. Be sure to thank God for those who colabor with you in this vital area.

   If you are uncertain where to turn for help with parenting, what direction does the Bible give you in Titus 2:3-4?

   Now make a list of those you could ask for help. Pray and then approach them. It's as simple as "I've got a question I'd like to ask you" or "I've got a situation I'd like your advice on."

What does the Bible say about seeking advice in...

...Proverbs 12:15?

...Proverbs 15:22?

...Proverbs 19:20?

...Proverbs 20:18?

2. If you're a more seasoned mom, one who has raised her children, realize God has an assignment for you. It's found in Titus 2:3-4 also. What does God want you to do?

How can you make yourself more available to other mothers?

Write down your personal child-raising principles, and seek ways to pass them on to others.

Wisdom from God

The habit of reading one chapter from the book of Proverbs every day—the chapter that corresponds with the date of the month—will make a difference not only each day, but in the direction your life takes as you walk on the path of daily wisdom. Stop now and read the "Proverbs for the day." Check here when done, and make note of one thing you learned, one change you must make, or some wisdom you gained for your life. _____

Ten Keys to Confident Child-Raising

1. *Teach your children*—Read these proverbs and note their messages to mothers.

    Proverbs 1:8—

    Proverbs 6:20—

    Proverbs 31:1—

    Now read Deuteronomy 6:6-7 and note this information:

    Who is to do the teaching?

    What is to be taught?

    Where is the teaching to take place?

    When is the teaching to take place?

What is the prerequisite for the teacher (verse 5)?

2. *Train your children*—The Bible clearly instructs parents to train their children for the Lord and His purposes. What does Proverbs 22:6 have to say?

In your book we considered the requirements for training children. How is...

...your heart of obedience?

...your heart of faith?

...your heart of dedication?

How can you turn up the heat in your heart if the fire is flickering and fading? List at least three steps or changes.

—

—

—

In chapter 7 you learned that Susanna Wesley was the mother of 19 children, including Christianity's famous brothers John and Charles. Susanna Wesley had a list of rules for raising and training her children. Before you read Mrs. Wesley's "Rules" on the next page, do you have written rules for child-raising? Do you have a set of guiding principles and practices? Are there certain scriptures upon which you base your child-raising? If not, start your own list by jotting down five principles you think are vital to raising healthy children.

—

—

—

—

—

Susanna Wesley's Rules for Raising Children

1. Allow no eating between meals.

2. Put all children in bed by eight o'clock.

3. Require them to take medicine without complaining.

4. Subdue self-will in a child and thus work together with God to save his soul.

5. Teach each one to pray as soon as he can speak.

6. Require all to be still during family worship.

7. Give them nothing that they cry for, and only that which they ask for politely.

8. To prevent lying, punish no fault which is first confessed and repented of.

9. Never allow a sinful act to go unpunished.

10. Never punish a child twice for a single offense.

11. Commend and reward good behavior.

12. Any attempt to please, even if poorly performed, should be commended.

13. Preserve property rights, even in the smallest matters.

14. Strictly observe all promises.

15. Require no daughter to work before she can read well.

16. Teach children to fear the rod.[14]

3. *Instruct them*—Scan through these instances of parental instruction. Briefly, what was the instruction?

   Proverbs 1:10-19—

   Proverbs 7:1-27—

   Proverbs 31:1-9—

   How seriously must you take God's instruction to you to instruct your children? Are any changes in your life called for?

4. *Correct them*—What do these proverbs teach you about correcting your children?

   Proverbs 13:24—

   Proverbs 23:13—

   Proverbs 19:18—

   Proverbs 29:15—

   Proverbs 22:15—

Just for Today

❧ *Just for today…*

❧ *Just for tomorrow…*

❧ *Just for this week…*

Living God's Plan

Read the "Living God's Plan" section in your book again. As you consider the contents of this chapter and "God's Guidelines for a Better Life," what principle or guideline really spoke to your heart...and what do you plan to do about it?

Love Your Children

In your copy of *Small Changes for a Better Life* read the chapter titled "Small Change #12—Love Your Children." What from this chapter meant the most to you, offered you the greatest challenge, or helped you make the small changes necessary for a better life?

Before beginning this lesson, look back at the previous one and copy the first four of the...

Ten Keys to Confident Child-Raising

1.

2.

3.

4.

5. *Cherish your children*—The "older women" of Titus 2:3
   were to admonish the younger women to "love their
   children" (verse 4). The word translated "love" means
   to have affection for or to cherish one's children. Take
   a minute to think back through the past week, through
   yesterday, even through this very morning. What are
   you doing in your relationships with your children that
   indicates to each of them that he or she is cherished?
   Try to think of several efforts, kindnesses, or choices
   you made that conveyed your love, fondness, and
   appreciation for your children. Even if your children
   are grown, go ahead and do the exercise. After all,
   "once a mother, always a mother." And if you have
   grandchildren, remember they too need to know of
   your love.

   Hannah is an outstanding example of a loving mother.
   Read her story now in 1 Samuel 1:9-11 and 20-28. What
   is your response to Hannah's willingness, if given a
   male child, to dedicate that child to the Lord?

Consider and answer these two questions:

—Does each of your children know he or she is cherished, well loved, and precious to you?

—In your heart, is each of your children "dedicated" to God?

6. *Take care of them*—Read about God's care for us in Matthew 6:25-32. This is a picture of the kind of care mothers should provide for their children. What steps did the Proverbs 31 woman take to care for the physical needs of her children (Proverbs 31:13-22)?

Do your efforts in providing for your children's physical needs measure up? Are there any changes, corrections, or additions that could be made? Be specific.

And just a note: One of your greatest means of caring for all aspects of your children's lives is through your faithful prayers. You just may well be the only person on earth who is praying for them. So whatever you do, do be faithful to pray.

7. *Pay attention to them*—Life can be busy and complicated. In the hustle and bustle of daily life and living, children can get lost in the shuffle. But your children need to know that they are a major priority. They grow up all too quickly, so while you have a chance, pay attention to your children. Do some or all of the following things this week. Check when they are done. Then journal or make a record of the responses of the children. And if there is no visible or verbal responses, that's okay.

_____ Read a story.

_____ Send an "I love you" note in their lunches.

_____ Take them on a special outing.

_____ Have an extra cuddle time while getting ready for bed.

_____ Take each one on a special outing alone.

_____ Hug your child three times a day and say "I love you!"

_____ Have a heart-to-heart talk with an older child, a "How are you really doing?" talk.

8. *Promote peace in your home*—Read again about "The Three C's" and look them up in the book of Proverbs.

    Casting lots—Proverbs 18:18. How might this practice help to keep the peace around your house?

    Correct—Proverbs 29:17. What seems to be the consistent, positive result of discipline according to...

    ...Proverbs 3:11-12?

    ...Proverbs 12:1?

    ...Proverbs 13:1?

    ...Proverbs 29:15?

    Casting out—Proverbs 22:10. As one scholar explains, "Disagreement...sometimes arises not from the facts of a situation but from a person with a wrong attitude, who makes mischief."[15] How might casting out help keep the peace around your house?

9. *Require respect from them*—Respect and honor of parents and authority is vital to raising godly children. What is the fifth of the Ten Commandments (Exodus 20:12)?

Look at Ephesians 6:1-3. Note how the apostle Paul personalized this command. What is its promise if obeyed?

What actions can hinder this training in respect (Ephesians 6:4)?

How high is your children's respect level when it comes to you as a parent? What first step can you take to raise that level?

10. *Be patient with them*—If you are a parent, you know raising children is not easy. There's no doubt patience plays a big role. Where does patience come from according to Galatians 5:22-23?

What does patience do according to...

...Proverbs 15:2?

...Proverbs 15:18?

...Proverbs 15:28?

...Proverbs 29:22?

Just for Today

❧ *Just for today…*

❧ *Just for tomorrow…*

❧ *Just for this week…*

Living God's Plan

Read the "Living God's Plan" section in your book again. As you consider the contents of this chapter and "God's Guidelines for a Better Life," what principle or guideline really spoke to your heart...and what do you plan to do about it?

Cultivate
Inner Beauty

In your copy of *Small Changes for a Better Life* read the chapter titled "Small Change #13—Cultivate Inner Beauty." What from this chapter meant the most to you, offered you the greatest challenge, or helped you make the small changes necessary for a better life?

Can you relate to the two women I heard discussing a television talk show on looks, beauty, appearance, and self-image? How many times a day do you think about your appearance? Note your nagging worries and concerns regarding your appearance.

Timeless Beauty Tips

1. *True beauty is internal*—If you are a child of God through Jesus Christ, Christ has secured for you what many refer to as your "position in Christ." What do these truths reveal about that position in Him?

      2 Corinthians 5:17—

      Ephesians 1:13—

      Ephesians 2:4-5—

      Colossians 1:13—

   How can remembering who you are in Christ correct any unworthy and untrue thoughts you may have about yourself?

2. *True beauty is enhanced by spiritual growth*—What harsh reality do you find in 2 Corinthians 4:16 regarding your physical body?

   Also, what refreshing truth do you find there?

   How does this take place (verse 18)?

Look at Proverbs 31:25 in your Bible and copy it here.

Can you name a handful of women you know who live out the truth of this scripture? Jot their names down. Thank God for them, and then pray for them. As a final assignment, write them each a note of appreciation and encouragement. It takes courage and discipline to live a godly life. You can be sure your notes will give them a ray of hope.

Meet Rebekah—

Here is beauty and "beauty" in action. Read Rebekah's story in Genesis 24:12-25. How does the Bible describe Rebekah's physical beauty?

How does the Bible detail the actions that revealed Rebekah's "beauty" of graciousness, mercy, compassion, energy, voluntary service, and helpfulness?

Other-oriented women do not selfishly and self-centeredly think about themselves. They have learned they cannot be consumed with themselves and with others at the same time. It is one or the other. How can you improve in following in Rebekah's beautiful footsteps of selflessness?

What does the New Testament say about the beauty of "good works" in 1 Timothy 2:9-10?

3. *True beauty is a matter of the heart*—In your Bible read 1 Peter 3:3-4. What strikes you most?

What is your response to these phrases? (Write in the
wording of these phrases from your favorite version of
the Bible.)

...the hidden person of the heart (verse 4)

...the incorruptible beauty (verse 4)

...a gentle and quiet spirit (verse 4)

...very precious in the sight of God (verse 4)

When it comes to your outward appearance, how does
1 Samuel 16:7 help?

Look at the following misuses of beauty. In each instance,
make note of the indicators of the heart of each woman and
how she used her beauty for evil.

Proverbs 5:3-8—

Proverbs 6:24-26—

Proverbs 7:5-21—

Proverbs 11:22—

What positive guidelines for your appearance can you draw
from these negative examples?

Checklist for Your Heart

Check out your "clothing." Does it match up to God's instruction? For every "spiritual garment," so to speak, list one way you can pay greater attention to it. (Look at each verse in your Bible. You may also substitute the wording from your favorite Bible.)

- Put on...tender mercies (Colossians 3:12).

- Put on...kindness (Colossians 3:12).

- Put on...humbleness of mind (Colossians 3:12).

- Put on...meekness (Colossians 3:12).

- Put on...longsuffering (Colossians 3:12).

- Put on...a gentle and quiet spirit (1 Peter 3:4).

- Put on...a cloak of humility (1 Peter 5:5).

What is the exhortation of Romans 13:14, and how would it help you with this "wardrobe" assignment?

Just for Today

An elderly Christian woman, distinguished for her youthful appearance, was asked what she used to preserve her charms. She replied sweetly,

> I used for the lips, truth; for the voice, prayer; for the eyes, pity; for the hand, charity; for the figure, uprightness; and for the heart, love.[16]

🌿 *Just for today...*

❧ *Just for tomorrow...*

❧ *Just for this week...*

Living God's Plan

Read the "Living God's Plan" section in your book again. As
you consider the contents of this chapter and "God's Guidelines for a Better Life," what principle or guideline really
spoke to your heart...and what do you plan to do about it?

Tend to Your Appearance

In your copy of *Small Changes for a Better Life* read the chapter titled "Small Change #14— Tend to Your Appearance." What from this chapter meant the most to you, offered you the greatest challenge, or helped you make the small changes necessary for a better life?

Before you begin this second lesson regarding your appearance, revisit the previous lesson and write out the biblical principles for appearance.

1—

2—

3—

More Timeless Beauty Tips

You've probably already been exposed to a lifetime of beauty tips. Indeed, every grocery store checkout line bombards you with magazine covers heralding some new beauty treatment, invention, or diet. And if you have daughters, you are entering Round 2 as they begin to delve into cosmetology. Truly it's a girl thing!

As one of God's women and a mom, you'll want to practice— and impart to your daughters—God's timeless principles and "beauty tips" for your appearance. Let's discover more about His plan regarding this most practical and daily issue in every woman's life.

4. *True beauty is also external*—We've been focusing on the internals of true beauty, on the inner person of the heart, and on nurturing a beautiful heart. As you begin this section of your study, look again in your Bible at 1 Timothy 2:9-10 concerning the externals of beauty. Keep it handy as you move through this section.

   Modesty—What dress standard do these verses set regarding modesty?

   1 Timothy 2:9—

   Titus 2:5—

   1 Peter 3:3—

How was a failure in modesty lived out in Proverbs 7:10?

Propriety—Look again at these verses and note their message about propriety.

    1 Timothy 2:9—

    Proverbs 31:25—

What is to be your motivation for propriety in your appearance according to Proverbs 31:30?

Humility was mentioned as an ingredient in propriety. What do these scriptures remind you about humility?

    Philippians 2:5,8—

    1 Peter 5:6—

    Colossians 3:12—

Moderation—Copy out 1 Timothy 2:9 from your Bible.

According to this verse, how were the women of Paul and Timothy's day obviously in violation of this principle of moderation?

You have already noted the element of self-control. Why would self-control be called for as you consider moderation in your appearance?

1 Timothy 2:9—

Proverbs 7:10—

Make a "Checklist for Moderation" drawn from the article by John MacArthur entitled "What's a Woman to Wear?"

As you consider God's description of the godly "older women" in Titus 2:3, where do you see modesty, propriety, and moderation fitting in?

The woman who is "reverent in behavior" is a woman who has a keen awareness that she is living her life in the presence of God. How do you think such a culti-vated awareness would make a difference in a wo-man's appearance?

What's a woman to wear? Are you using this checklist for your daily grooming? And how would doing so make a difference? (Also don't fail to share this biblical checklist with your daughters.)

Check yourself...

> ...for modesty—"Do I look pure?" "Am I wearing too little?"
>
> ...for propriety—"Is my appearance reflecting a proper image of a woman of God?"
>
> ...for moderation—"Would my appearance cause someone to stumble?" "Am I wearing too much?"
>
> ...for wisdom—The wise woman will pass this test.

Practical Beauty Tips

Dress up—Esther was "Queen Esther." As you read Esther 5:1-2, how was she appropriately and properly attired for her status as queen and for the nature of her business (see Esther 4:8) as she stood before her husband, the king?

The Proverbs 31 woman was a fabric merchant (Proverbs 31:24) and an artisan. How was her clothing appropriate and proper for her status (verse 22)?

How do the examples of these two wise and godly women—Esther and the Proverbs 31 woman—guide you in your dressing up...versus today's current tendency to dress down?

Fix up—How do these scriptures encourage you to think of others, even in the matter of your appearance?

Romans 12:10—

Philippians 2:3-4—

Clean up—How does Proverbs 27:9 speak of the results of our efforts to clean up and spruce up a little?

Look up—Great change is commenced by praying about everything, even about what we wear. What kind of heart looks up and is concerned with God's standard and approval regarding clothing and appearance?

1 Peter 3:4—

1 Peter 3:15—(To sanctify means to enshrine, to love, to obey, and to set apart as a priority.)

Just for Today

❧ *Just for today...*

❧ *Just for tomorrow...*

❧ *Just for this week...*

Living God's Plan

Read the "Living God's Plan" section in your book again. As you consider the contents of this chapter and "God's Guidelines for a Better Life," what principle or guideline really spoke to your heart...and what do you plan to do about it?

Watch What You Eat

In your copy of *Small Changes for a Better Life* read the chapter titled "Small Change #15—Watch What You Eat." What from this chapter meant the most to you, offered you the greatest challenge, or helped you make the small changes necessary for a better life?

The Bible has a lot to say about different kinds of appetites, about desires. Many of these desires are for the wrong things. God's Word helps us keep our desires under control. As we live out God's plan, we are guided to choose the right things, which in turn leads to a better and more satisfying life. There are many appetites—materialism, the craving of worldly things, sensual lusts—that affect our habits. But for this lesson we'll focus on one aspect of appetite—food.

Better Eating God's Way

Copy 1 Corinthians 10:31 from your version of the Bible. Then write out Rule 1 for better eating God's way.

Rule 1—

> First, *the physical*—Have you ever tried to start your car and in the process flooded the engine with too much gas? That's what happens when you "flood" your body with too much food at one time. God created you, and He knows what's best. That's why knowing and paying attention to His guidelines regarding food is important.
>
> From the beginning of the Bible, God has been interested in what His children eat and do not eat. He gave specific instructions to protect His people through dietary and hygienic restrictions. But more importantly, He was stressing obedience to Him and the separation of His people from idolatrous nations.[17] In the fewest words possible, what instructions were given to the following people?
>
> Adam and Eve in Genesis 2:16-17—
>
> The Israelites in Leviticus 11:1-2—

God is also interested in how much His children eat. What are a few of His guidelines, and what happens when we ignore them?

Proverbs 23:20-21—

Proverbs 25:16—

Everyone has overeaten at some time. Describe such a time for you and its physical effects. In other words, how did you feel?

Next, *the financial*—Revisit Proverbs 23:20-21. What does it say will happen financially to the one who drinks and eats too much?

Now, an exercise—Look back over this past week. How much money did you and your family spend on food?

How much money did you spend on eating out and bringing home fast foods?

What does this reveal about your family's eating habits?

What does this reveal about your family's financial habits?

List several ways you can make food a less costly item in your family budget.

—

—

—

And *the spiritual*—Where can a Christian go for help with an eating problem according to...

...Galatians 5:16?

...Galatians 5:22-23?

What spiritual help does Romans 13:14 give regarding any and all appetites?

What practical help does Romans 13:14 give you about such issues as what you put on your grocery list, purchase at the store, bring home, place in the cupboard and pantry, and make readily available for your moments of weakness? (In other words, are you planning ahead and providing for sinful gratification? Are you planning to overindulge ahead of time?)

Daniel was a man in the Bible who showed a heart for obeying God in the area of food. Map out the scenes and the order of events in...

> ...Daniel 1:3-5

> ...Daniel 1:8-14

> ...Daniel 1:15-16

Read again the quote by Elisabeth Elliot on the page preceding the first page of this chapter in your book. How do you think greater discipline in the area of food can strengthen your "spiritual fiber"?

The seven deadly sins, according to Thomas Aquinas, are:

Envy	Lust	Sloth
Anger	Greed	Gluttony
Pride		

Another exercise—Look back over this past week. How much time did you and your family spend purchasing, preparing, and eating snack foods? Shine a spotlight on your habits and patterns. Look for the excesses and practices that indicate a lack of control. Remember, bad habits are like a comfortable bed...easy to get into but hard to get out of, and you are looking for change.

A Prayer for a Better Life

Lord, may a lifestyle of physical fatigue, financial folly, spiritual deadening, and the practical misuse of time not be true of me! Help me live my life in a better way—in Your way. Amen.

Are the words of this prayer the words of your heart? Pray them now...and every day...until the truths taught in God's Word about food are yours. Then you will be a woman who is on the way to a better life.

Just for Today

❧ *Just for today…*

❧ *Just for tomorrow…*

❧ *Just for this week…*

Living God's Plan

Read the "Living God's Plan" section in your book again. As you consider the contents of this chapter and "God's Guidelines for a Better Life," what principle or guideline really spoke to your heart...and what do you plan to do about it?

Eat Just Enough

In your copy of *Small Changes for a Better Life* read the chapter titled "Small Change #16— Eat Just Enough." What from this chapter meant the most to you, offered you the greatest challenge, or helped you make the small changes necessary for a better life?

More on Better Eating God's Way!

As you begin this lesson, copy out Rule 1 from the previous lesson. Then, as you work your way through the remaining rules for better eating God's way, record each rule.

Rule 1—

Rule 2—

Read Proverbs 30:8-9, a guiding principle for every woman who wants to know and live out God's plan. How do these verses define moderation in food for you?

What is the danger of too much?

What is the danger of too little?

According to the New Testament, what are the basics of life (1 Timothy 6:6-8)?

Verse 6—

Verse 8—

Where are you in the area of contentment? Are you overly concerned about food...or are you content with just enough (see Proverbs 30:8)? Please explain your answer.

What is one physical effect of eating more than just enough?

Unless you are in the percentage of the world's people who are deprived of the basics of living, you have much to be thankful for. Pause now and offer up a prayer of thanksgiving to the Lord.

Rule 3—

Copy Proverbs 25:16 here. Then put it into your own words.

Look again at the story of Eve in Genesis 3:1-6. Then read Genesis 2:16. How did Eve choose her own way regarding eating and thus violate Rule 3?

What lessons can you learn from Eve about trusting God for your daily bread?

Rule 4—

Addictions are terrible things. Alcohol. Tobacco. Drugs. Food. These are problem areas for many people. Yes, food is included. When we come to the table and cannot control our eating habits, we must face the truth that we have a problem with food. Write out Paul's words of wisdom in 1 Corinthians 6:12:

Are there any appetites mastering you? What steps can you take to overcome them so Paul's battle cry applies to your life too?

What great resource is available to you according to 2 Corinthians 12:9?

Rule 5—

We have now come full circle. We started with 1 Corinthians 10:31 in our last lesson, and now we end with that same pivotal verse. Write it out again here.

Here in this lesson, under Rule 4, are two questions related to the steps you could take to overcome any addictions and appetites. How will 1 Corinthians 10:31 help bring about change?

Better Living God's Way

As was noted in the previous lesson regarding God's servant Daniel, the matter of food was Step 1 in God's preparation of him as a man whose spiritual fiber would be rigorously tested later on. Daniel's life, as is everyone's, was one rigorous trial after another. How do these scriptures point you to a way of life that goes beyond food to master the "all things" and the "anythings" and the "everythings" of life?

1 Corinthians 6:12—

1 Corinthians 6:19-20—

1 Corinthians 9:27—

1 Corinthians 10:23—

1 Corinthians 10:31—

As you thread the teachings of these scriptures together, share…

…how you are more motivated to run the race for the prize of the upward call of God in Christ Jesus (Philippians 3:14).

…how you are more prepared to run the race.

…how you are more informed to run the race.

What is the first thing you must change or gain control over so you can better run the race of your life?

Just for Today

Just for today…

🌿 *Just for tomorrow...*

🌿 *Just for this week...*

Living God's Plan

Read the "Living God's Plan" section in your book again. As you consider the contents of this chapter and "God's Guidelines for a Better Life," what principle or guideline really spoke to your heart...and what do you plan to do about it?

Grow in Discipline

In your copy of *Small Changes for a Better Life* read the chapter titled "Small Change #17— Grow in Discipline." What from this chapter meant the most to you, offered you the greatest challenge, or helped you make the small changes necessary for a better life?

God's Take on Discipline

Recognize that discipline is a spiritual issue—Read the complete list of the fruit of the Spirit in Galatians 5:22-23. How important is self-control to the other fruit mentioned in these verses?

Readily acknowledge sin—We are told many times in the Bible to "walk" in a particular manner. What do these verses say about your walk?

Galatians 5:16—

Ephesians 5:15—

Ephesians 4:1—

Colossians 4:5—

Ephesians 5:2—

1 John 1:7—

Ephesians 5:8—

3 John 4—

Key in now on Galatians 5:16. How does walking in the Spirit help in the battle against the flesh?

Describe the battle waged by every believer between the flesh and the Spirit as detailed in Galatians 5:17.

Write out these verses to get a better picture of the full effects and consequences of sin when it comes to the ministry of the Holy Spirit in your life.

Ephesians 4:30—

1 Thessalonians 5:19—

How do these two scriptures and situations impress upon you the importance and the way to keep a clean slate with God?

David shows us how—What did David look for as a result of his confession of his sins (Psalm 51:12)?

What desire and fruit followed David's confession and forgiveness (Psalm 51:13)?

Discipline is an act of the will—How did Paul willfully deal with discipline in his life (1 Corinthians 9:27)?

Once again, how can you willfully deal with discipline in your life according to...

...Romans 13:14?

...1 Corinthians 6:12?

...1 Corinthians 9:25?

...1 Corinthians 9:27?

...Colossians 3:5?

...1 Thessalonians 4:3?

...2 Timothy 2:22?

...1 Peter 2:11?

God is faithful to tell His children exactly what they are to do and not do. It is our obedience to Him that births, builds, and strengthens discipline. Are you faithful to follow through, carry out, and obey God's wisdom? What area(s) of personal discipline are you now working to improve? What specifically are you doing to deal with it?

Rejoice with each victory—You can probably identify with Paul in his struggle. Read Romans 7:13-25 and briefly relate how Paul describes the battle every believer is fighting against his or her flesh.

Now that you are more aware of the struggle, what hope of victory does Paul give in Romans 8:1-2?

What is your assurance of victory (1 John 5:4)?

Once again, who has victory (1 John 5:5)?

Remember that discipline mirrors maturity—Each step of self-control and self-discipline leads to greater spiritual strength and maturity. As a result of victory in our Lord Jesus Christ (1 Corinthians 15:57), what resolves should you now have (1 Corinthians 15:58)?

—

—

—

What ability comes with maturity according to Hebrews 5:14?

In verse 14, what activity makes this ability possible?

What can you do today "by reason of use"—by constant use and practice or habit—to develop and train yourself and your senses (sight, sound, touch, and so forth) to discern in your daily life what is right and wrong?

A Better Life Requires Discipline

Meet Eve—Please reread Genesis 3:1-7 and fill in the spaces with the corresponding verses.

Eve talked too much, verse_____

Eve held back too little, verse_____

Eve wanted too much, verse_____

Eve ate too much, verse_____

Knowing what you've now learned, if you had been in Eve's position, how would (Lord willing!) you have handled the situation differently?

Now Meet Abigail...Again—Scan 1 Samuel 25 in your Bible. List the steps of wisdom you observe Abigail taking in her difficult situation. What lessons can Abigail teach you about your life situation?

Just for Today

❧ *Just for today...*

❧ *Just for tomorrow...*

❧ *Just for this week...*

Living God's Plan

Read the "Living God's Plan" section in your book again. As you consider the contents of this chapter and "God's Guidelines for a Better Life," what principle or guideline really spoke to your heart...and what do you plan to do about it?

Work with Diligence

 In your copy of *Small Changes for a Better Life* read the chapter titled "Small Change #18—Work with Diligence." What from this chapter meant the most to you, offered you the greatest challenge, or helped you make the small changes necessary for a better life?

God's Plan for Diligence

Read the verses on diligence noted in your book, and then state how you can become more diligent in each area.

- Finances—

- Livelihood—

- Income and productivity—

- Contribution to society—

- Outcome—

- Comfort—

- Household—

155

Look again at the wise woman's diligence. Check the areas where you can become more diligent in your household. Make notes detailing how you plan to get started.

> ...rises while it is yet night
>
> ...girds herself with strength
>
> ...strengthens her arms
>
> ...works into the night
>
> ...does not eat the bread of idleness

What will be the results of your diligence?

1.

2.

3.

4.

5.

Motivators for Diligence

Awareness of the brevity of life—What are the Bible's remarks on the brevity of life in the following scriptures?

> Job 7:6—
>
> 1 Peter 1:24—

Note the teaching of the following scriptures. Remember that whether we acknowledge the brevity of life or not, we have a choice. We can either follow the negative models of...

> ...Proverbs 6:10-11
>
> ...Proverbs 20:4
>
> ...Proverbs 21:25

or we can follow the positive models of...

   ...Proverbs 22:29

   ...Proverbs 31:13

   ...Proverbs 31:15

   ...Proverbs 31:16

   ...Proverbs 31:17

   ...Proverbs 31:18

   ...Proverbs 31:19

   ...Proverbs 31:21

What will your choice be? List three things you'll do to get started right away.

   —

   —

   —

Awareness of the purpose of life—Leaf through chapter 3 in your book, the chapter on "Purpose." As a quick refresher on purpose, what do the following verses remind you about God's purpose for your life?

Ephesians 2:10—

1 Corinthians 10:31—

Awareness of stewardship—How do these scriptures motivate you to be diligent about your stewardship?

Matthew 25:23—

Luke 12:42-44—

1 Corinthians 4:2—

2 Corinthians 5:10—

Awareness of time—Read Ephesians 5:15-16 and analyze your average day. When do your peaks and valleys normally occur? Are they fairly consistent each day...or do things come up that alter a predictable pattern (things like late-night engagements, sick children who need care through the night)? Hopefully these altered plans are not the norm. Once you are aware of your highs and lows of energy, write the times they occur below. Then assign appropriate tasks for each period for tomorrow or this next week.

Time of high energy level _____

Activities for this period of my day:

—

—

—

Times of low energy level _____

Activities for this period of my day:

—

—

—

Evaluate your productivity at the end of the day and the week as a result of seeking to work more diligently with your time.

An Example of Diligence

Take a few minutes and scan chapter 2 of the book of Ruth and jot down what you observe of Ruth's diligence and what impresses you most. As we noted, Ruth is "an example of diligence." Now list two ways you can follow in her footsteps.

Just for Today

❧ *Just for today...*

❧ *Just for tomorrow...*

❧ *Just for this week...*

Living God's Plan

Read the "Living God's Plan" section in your book again. As you consider the contents of this chapter and "God's Guidelines for a Better Life," what principle or guideline really spoke to your heart...and what do you plan to do about it?

Living God's Plan for Life

You have worked long and hard to find God's truth. You have learned much about God's plan. And you have made many small changes along the way. Look at the Table of Contents in the front of the book for a summary of the life-topics you have encountered in this study. Then write out the three most important changes you have made or are ready to make in living out God's plan for a better life.

—

—

—

May God richly bless you as you follow
His plan for a better life.

Leading a Bible Study Discussion Group

*W*hat a privilege it is to lead a Bible study! And what joy and excitement await you as you delve into the Word of God and help others to discover its life-changing truths. If God has called you to lead a Bible study group, I know you'll be spending much time in prayer and planning and giving much thought to being an effective leader. I also know that taking the time to read through the following tips will help you navigate the challenges of leading a Bible study discussion group and enjoy the effort and opportunity.

The Leader's Roles

As a Bible study group leader, you'll find your role changing back and forth from *leader* to *cheerleader* to *lover* to *referee* during the course of a session.

Since you're the leader, group members will look to you to be the *leader* guiding them through the material. So be well prepared. In fact, be over-prepared so that you know the material better than any group member does. Start your study early in the week and let its message simmer all week long. (You might even work several lessons ahead so that you have in mind the big picture and the overall direction of the study.) Be ready to share some additional gems that your group members wouldn't have discovered on their own. That extra insight from your study time — or that comment from a wise Bible teacher or scholar, that clever saying, that keen observation from another believer, and even an appropriate joke — adds an element of fun and keeps Bible study from becoming routine, monotonous, and dry.

Next, be ready to be the group's *cheerleader*. Your energy and enthusiasm for the task at hand can be contagious. It can also stimulate people to get more involved in their personal study as well as in the group discussion.

Third, be the *lover*, the one who shows a genuine concern for the members of the group. You're the one who will establish the atmosphere of the group. If you laugh and have fun, the group members will laugh and have fun. If you hug, they will hug. If you care, they will care. If you share, they will share. If you love, they will love. So pray every day to love the women God has placed in your group. Ask Him to show you how to love them with His love.

Finally, as the leader, you'll need to be the *referee* on occasion. That means making sure everyone has an equal opportunity to speak. That's easier to do when you operate under the assumption that every member of the group has something worthwhile to contribute. So, trusting that the Lord has taught each person during the week, act on that assumption.

Leader, cheerleader, lover, and referee — these four roles of the leader may make the task seem overwhelming. But that's not bad if it keeps you on your knees praying for your group.

A Good Start

Beginning on time, greeting people warmly, and opening in prayer gets the study off to a good start. Know what you want to have happen during your time together and make sure those things get done. That kind of order means comfort for those involved.

Establish a format and let the group members know what that format is. People appreciate being in a Bible study that focuses on the Bible. So keep the discussion on the topic and move the group through the questions. Tangents are often hard to avoid — and even harder to rein in. So be sure to focus on the answers to questions about the specific passage at hand. After all, the purpose of the group is Bible study!

Finally, as someone has accurately observed, "Personal growth is one of the by-products of any effective small group. This growth is achieved when people are recognized and accepted by others. The more friendliness, mutual trust, respect, and warmth exhibited, the more likely that the member will find pleasure in the group, and, too, the more likely she will work hard toward the accomplishment of the group's goals. The effective leader will strive to reinforce desirable traits" (source unknown).

A Dozen Helpful Tips

Here is a list of helpful suggestions for leading a Bible study discussion group:

1. Arrive early, ready to focus fully on others and give of yourself. If you have to do any last-minute preparation, review, re-grouping, or praying, do it in the car. Don't dash in, breathless, harried, late, still tweaking your plans.

2. Check out your meeting place in advance. Do you have everything you need — tables, enough chairs, a blackboard, hymnals if you plan to sing, coffee, etc.?

3. Greet each person warmly by name as she arrives. After all, you've been praying for these women all week long, so let each VIP know that you're glad she's arrived.

4. Use name tags for at least the first two or three weeks.

5. Start on time no matter what — even if only one person is there!

6. Develop a pleasant but firm opening statement. You might say, "This lesson was great! Let's get started so we can enjoy all of it!" or "Let's pray before we begin our lesson."

7. Read the questions, but don't hesitate to reword them on occasion. Rather than reading an entire paragraph of instructions, for instance, you might say, "Question 1 asks us to list some ways that Christ displayed humility. Lisa, please share one way Christ displayed humility."

8. Summarize or paraphrase the answers given. Doing so will keep the discussion focused on the topic, eliminate digressions, help avoid or clear up any misunderstandings of the text, and keep each group member aware of what the others are saying.

9. Keep moving and don't add any of your own questions to the discussion time. It's important to get through the study guide questions. So if a cut-and-dried answer is called for, you don't need to comment with anything other than a "thank you." But when the question asks for an opinion or an application (for instance, "How

can this truth help us in our marriages?" or "How do *you* find time for your quiet time?"), let all who want to contribute do so.

10. Affirm each person who contributes, especially if the contribution was very personal, painful to share, or a quiet person's rare statement. Acknowledge everyone who shares a hero by saying something like "Thank you for sharing that insight from your own life" or "We certainly appreciate what God has taught you. Thank you for letting us in on it."

11. Watch your watch, put a clock right in front of you, or consider using a timer. Pace the discussion so that you meet your cut-off time, especially if you want time to pray. Stop at the designated time even if you haven't finished the lesson. Remember that everyone has worked through the study once; you are simply going over it again.

12. End on time. You can only make friends with your group members by ending on time or even a little early! Besides, members of your group have the next item on their agenda to attend to — picking up children from the nursery, babysitter, or school; heading home to tend to matters there; running errands; getting to bed; or spending some time with their husbands. So let them out *on time!*

Five Common Problems

In any group, you can anticipate certain problems. Here are some common ones that can arise, along with helpful solutions:

1. *The incomplete lesson* — Right from the start, establish the policy that if someone has not done the lesson, it is best for her not to answer the questions. But do try to include her responses to questions that ask for opinions or experiences. Everyone can share some thoughts in reply to a question like "Reflect on what you know about both athletic and spiritual training, and then share what you consider to be the essential elements of training oneself in godliness."

2. *The gossip* — The Bible clearly states that gossiping is wrong, so you don't want to allow it in your group. Set a high and strict standard by saying, "I am not comfortable with this conversation," or "We [not *you*] are gossiping, ladies. Let's move on."

3. *The talkative member* — Here are three scenarios and some possible solutions for each.

   a. The problem talker may be talking because she has done her homework and is excited about something she has to share. She may also know more about the subject than the others and, if you cut her off, the rest of the group may suffer.

      SOLUTION: Respond with a comment like: "Sarah, you are making very valuable contributions. Let's see if we can get some reactions from the others," or "I know Sarah can answer this. She's really done her homework. How about some of the rest of you?"

   b. The talkative member may be talking because she has *not* done her homework and wants to contribute, but she has no boundaries.

SOLUTION: Establish at the first meeting that those who have not done the lesson do not contribute except on opinion or application questions. You may need to repeat this guideline at the beginning of each session.

c. The talkative member may want to be heard whether or not she has anything worthwhile to contribute.

SOLUTION: After subtle reminders, be more direct, saying, "Betty, I know you would like to share your ideas, but let's give others a chance. I'll call on you later."

4. *The quiet member* — Here are two scenarios and possible solutions.

a. The quiet member wants the floor but somehow can't get the chance to share.

SOLUTION: Clear the path for the quiet member by first watching for clues that she wants to speak (moving to the edge of her seat, looking as if she wants to speak, perhaps even starting to say something) and then saying, "Just a second. I think Chris wants to say something." Then, of course, make her a hero!

b. The quiet member simply doesn't want the floor.

SOLUTION: "Chris, what answer do you have on question 2?" or "Chris, what do you think about...?" Usually after a shy person has contributed a few times, she will become more confident and more ready to share. Your role is to provide an opportunity where there is *no* risk of a wrong answer. But occasionally a group member will tell you that she would rather not be called on.

Honor her request, but from time to time ask her privately if she feels ready to contribute to the group discussions.

In fact, give all your group members the right to pass. During your first meeting, explain that any time a group member does not care to share an answer, she may simply say, "I pass." You'll want to repeat this policy at the beginning of every group session.

5. *The wrong answer* — Never tell a group member that she has given a wrong answer, but at the same time never let a wrong answer go by.

SOLUTION: Either ask if someone else has a different answer or ask additional questions that will cause the right answer to emerge. As the women get closer to the right answer, say, "We're getting warmer! Keep thinking! We're almost there!"

Learning from Experience

Immediately after each Bible study session, evaluate the group discussion time using this checklist. You may also want a member of your group (or an assistant or trainee or outside observer) to evaluate you periodically.

May God strengthen — and encourage! — you as you assist others in the discovery of His many wonderful truths.

Notes

1. Donald S. Whitney, *Ten Questions to Diagnose Your Spiritual Health* (Colorado Springs: NavPress, 2001), p. 93.

2. Derek Kidner, *The Proverbs* (Downers Grove, IL: InterVarsity Press, 1973), p. 118.

3. Charles W. Turner, *Studies in Proverbs* (Grand Rapids, MI: Baker Book House, 1981), pp. 33-34.

4. Robert L. Alden, *Proverbs, A Commentary on an Ancient Book of Timeless Advice* (Grand Rapids, MI: Baker Book House, 1995), p. 32.

5. Louis Goldberg, *Wisdom for Living* (Chicago: The Moody Bible Institute, 1983), p. 44.

6. Leroy Eims, *Wisdom from Above for Living Here Below* (Wheaton, IL: Victor Books, 1981), p. 43.

7. The Tract League, Grand Rapids, MI 49544-1390.

8. Elizabeth George, *Life Management for Busy Women* (Eugene, OR: Harvest House Publishers, 2002), pp. 31-32.

9. Charles F. Pfeiffer and Everett F. Harrison, eds., *The Wycliffe Bible Commentary* (Chicago: Moody Press, 1973), p. 1446.

10. Mark Porter, *The Time of Your Life* (Wheaton, IL: Victor Books, 1983), p. 179.

11. Edward R. Dayton and Ted W. Engstrom, quoting Peter Drucker, *Strategy for Living* (Glendale, CA: G/L Publications, 1978), p. 179.

12. Benjamin R. DeJong, *Uncle Ben's Quotebook* (Grand Rapids, MI: Baker Book House, 1977), p. 199.

13. Elizabeth George, *A Woman After God's Own Heart®* (Eugene, OR: Harvest House Publishers, 1997), pp. 169-70.

14. Eleanor L. Doan, *The Speaker's Sourcebook*, quoting *Home Life* (Grand Rapids, MI: Zondervan Publishing House, 1977), p. 50.

15. Kidner, *The Proverbs,* p. 148.

16. Doan, *The Speaker's Sourcebook,* quoting Jerry Fleishman, p. 23.

17. John MacArthur, *The MacArthur Study Bible* (Nashville: Word Publishing, 1997), p. 168.

About the Author

Elizabeth George is a bestselling author who has more than 3.4 million books in print. She's a popular speaker at Christian women's events. Her passion is to teach the Bible in a way that changes women's lives. For information about Elizabeth's books or speaking ministry, to sign up for her mailings, or to share how God has used this book in your life, please write to Elizabeth at:

Elizabeth George
P.O. Box 2879
Belfair, WA 98528

Toll-free fax/phone:
1-800-542-4611
www.ElizabethGeorge.com

A Woman After God's Own Heart® Study Series

Bible Studies for Busy Women

God wrote the Bible to change hearts and lives. Every study in this series is written with that in mind—and is especially focused on helping Christian women know how God desires for them to live."

—Elizabeth George

Sharing wisdom gleaned from more than 20 years as a women's Bible study teacher, Elizabeth h prepared insightful lessons that can be completed in 15 to 20 minutes per day. Each lesson includ thought-provoking questions, insights, Bible-study tips, instructions for leading a discussion group, a a "heart response" section to make the Bible passage more personal.

978-0-7369-0816-0

978-0-7369-0489-6

978-0-7369-0290-8

978-0-7369-0818-4

978-0-7369-0300-4

978-0-7369-0301-1

978-0-7369-0289-2

978-0-7369-0665-4

978-0-7369-0498-8

978-0-7369-0490-2

HARVEST HOUSE PUBLISHERS
EUGENE, OREGON 97402
www.harvesthousepublishers.com

Remarkable Women of the Bible

by Elizabeth George

Experience God's life-changing power as the women of the Bible experienced it.

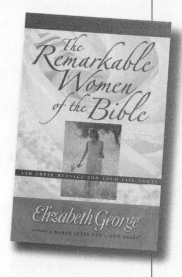

Come see how God enabled ordinary women to live extraordinary lives. How? By turning their weaknesses into strengths, their sorrows into joys, and their despair into hope. Along the way, you'll learn great truths about God Himself...

- from Eve you'll see God is faithful, even when you fail
- from Sarah you'll find God always keeps His promises
- from Rebekah you'll discover God has a plan for your life
- from Mary you'll learn God will always care for you.

What made these women—and many others—so remarkable? They loved God passionately, looked to Him in life's daily challenges, and yielded to His transforming grace. And you can enjoy God's miraculous work in your life today...by following in their footsteps.

Also available for supplemental study is *The Remarkable Women of the Bible Growth and Study Guide.*

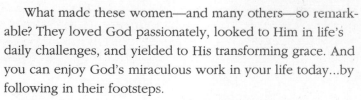

Books by Elizabeth George

- Beautiful in God's Eyes
- Life Management for Busy Women
- Loving God with All Your Mind
- A Mom After God's Own Heart
- Powerful Promises for Every Woman
- The Remarkable Women of the Bible
- Small Changes for a Better Life
- A Wife After God's Own Heart
- A Woman After God's Own Heart®
- A Woman After God's Own Heart® Deluxe Edition
- A Woman's Call to Prayer
- A Woman's High Calling
- A Woman's Walk with God
- A Young Woman After God's Own Heart
- A Young Woman's Call to Prayer
- A Young Woman's Walk with God

Children's Books

- God's Wisdom for Little Girls

Study Guides

- Beautiful in God's Eyes Growth & Study Guide
- Life Management for Busy Women Growth & Study Guide
- Loving God with All Your Mind Growth & Study Guide
- A Mom After God's Own Heart Growth & Study Guide
- Powerful Promises for Every Woman Growth & Study Guide
- The Remarkable Women of the Bible Growth & Study Guide
- Small Changes for a Better Life Growth & Study Guide
- A Wife After God's Own Heart Growth & Study Guide
- A Woman After God's Own Heart® Growth & Study Guide
- A Woman's Call to Prayer Growth & Study Guide
- A Woman's High Calling Growth & Study Guide
- A Woman's Walk with God Growth & Study Guide

Books by Jim & Elizabeth George

- God Loves His Precious Children
- God's Wisdom for Little Boys

Books by Jim George

- God's Man of Influence
- A Husband After God's Own Heart
- A Man After God's Own Heart
- The Remarkable Prayers of the Bible
- The Remarkable Prayers of the Bible Growth & Study Guide
- A Young Man After God's Own Heart